PIONEERS OF SCIENCE

JAMES WATT

Douglas McTavish

Pioneers of Science

Archimedes
Alexander Graham Bell
Karl Benz
Marie Curie
Thomas Edison
Albert Einstein
Michael Faraday
Alexander Fleming
Galileo
Edward Jenner
Joseph Lister
Guglielmo Marconi
Isaac Newton
Louis Pasteur
Leonardo da Vinci
James Watt

Series and book editor Rosemary Ashley
Designer David Armitage

First published in 1992 by
Wayland (Publishers) Ltd
61 Western Road, Hove
East Sussex BN3 1JD, England

© Copyright 1992 Wayland (Publishers) Limited

British Library Cataloguing in Publication Data
McTavish, Douglas
   James Watt. – (Pioneers of science)
   I. Title   II. Series
   621.1092
   ISBN 0–7502–0319–6

Typeset by DP Press Ltd, Sevenoaks, Kent
Printed in Italy by Rotolito Lombarda S.p.A.
Bound in France by A.G.M.

Contents

1 Early Years

James Watt was born on 19 January 1736 in Greenock, a town on the River Clyde in Scotland. His father had originally trained as a carpenter, although he branched out into a number of other businesses, including house construction and shipbuilding. He later became a general merchant and part-owner of several ships.

James was a sickly child who suffered frequent bouts of illness. Because he was so delicate, he was unable to go to school until he was ten years old. Having spent a large part of his young life being nursed by his mother through various illnesses, James found his fellow pupils boisterous and noisy. Perhaps because of this, he did not at first do well at school.

The house in Greenock, Scotland, in which James Watt was born.

While still a schoolboy in his teens, Watt was interested in experimenting, and in developing his abilities as a craftsman.

After a couple of years he moved to his local grammar school. He was happier there and his work immediately began to improve, especially in mathematics. His father seems to have passed on to James his early training as a craftsman. While he was still at school, James had a workbench and forge which he used to develop the skills he would need in his chosen career – making scientific instruments.

The main entrance of Glasgow University. Watt made a number of friends among the teachers at the University and one of them, Robert Dick, suggested he should go to London to complete his training as an instrument-maker.

At the age of eighteen, James travelled to the nearby city of Glasgow, to begin his training. In those days, instrument-makers were called upon to do much more than produce scientific instruments. If someone designed a new type of machine, for example, an instrument-maker might be asked to build the machine using the inventor's drawings. Watt's first master in Glasgow made, among other things, scientific instruments, drawing implements, cutlery and fishing tackle, and he also repaired musical instruments.

A relative of the Watt family, George Muirhead, was a professor at Glasgow University, and he introduced young James to some of his fellow teachers. Despite his late start at school, James enjoyed reading and had gained a good deal of knowledge from books. The teachers and professors he met in Glasgow were impressed by his knowledge and his enquiring mind. One of them, Robert Dick, taught natural philosophy, a subject similar to what we now call physics.

He suggested that James should go to London to train, because that was where the best instrument-makers were to be found. James took his advice and, after persuading his father to pay for the trip, he set out for London in June 1755.

James had been given a letter of introduction from Robert Dick to James Short, a fellow Scotsman, who was an instrument-maker in the Strand. However, Short could not give him a job, and James was no more successful when he approached other instrument-makers. The problem was that organizations known as trade guilds governed the way in which many trades, including instrument-making, were carried on. James had not served as an apprentice and so he could not be employed, and he could not become an apprentice because he was too old.

These craftsmen are making musical instruments. In Watt's day, people who made scientific instruments also made and repaired musical instruments, cutlery and fishing tackle.

Eventually, with Short's help, James found a master, John Morgan, who would teach him for a year at a fee of twenty guineas. James knew he had a year of hard work ahead of him; the knowledge and skills he needed would normally have taken four or five years to learn. He devoted himself to his studies, working until nine at night and rarely going out to enjoy himself. At the end of his training he was confident that he would be able to find work anywhere, and he returned to Scotland.

After spending some time at home in Greenock he moved to Glasgow where, in 1757, he began his first job. The university asked him to clean and repair a collection of astronomical instruments (for studying stars). He was provided with a workshop, and this soon became a meeting place for a group of men who shared Watt's interest in

Dr Joseph Black was Professor of Chemistry and of Medicine at Glasgow University. His studies into the properties of heat influenced Watt's work. He was impressed by Watt's intelligence and curiosity, and the two men became great friends.

natural philosophy. Among them were Joseph Black and John Robison, both of whom taught at the university. At first these men were surprised by Watt's knowledge and curiosity. Their surprise changed to respect and after a short time the three became lifelong friends.

During the next few years, Watt became quite prosperous. He moved to a new workshop and took on a partner to help him with his growing workload, which included making not only scientific instruments but guitars, flutes, harps and bagpipes. Then, in 1763, Watt was given a job that was to change the course of his life.

Watt's workshop at Glasgow University became the meeting place of a circle of friends who enjoyed discussing scientific subjects. Among them was Joseph Black (seated on the right).

9

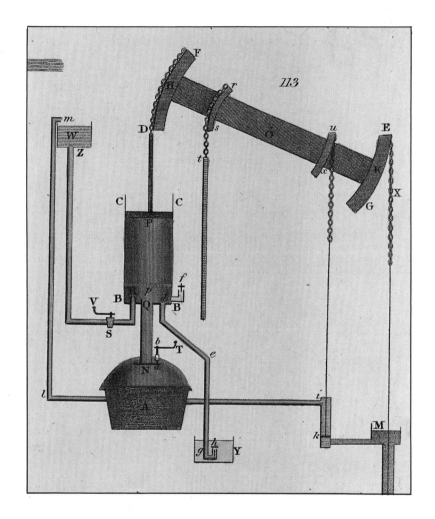

This diagram shows a Newcomen atmospheric engine used for mine-pumping. Steam produced by the boiler (A) forced up the piston (P) and the right-hand side of the wooden beam rocked downwards. When the steam in the cylinder was condensed to water, a partial vacuum was created beneath the piston, and atmospheric pressure forced it downwards through the cylinder. This caused the beam to rock again, lifting the right-hand side which was attached by rods to the apparatus that pumped water from the mine.

Watt's task was to repair a working model of a steam-engine that was used in the natural philosophy class at the university. The so-called atmospheric engine, on which the model was based, had been invented in about 1712 by Thomas Newcomen, an ironmonger in Devon. The machine's purpose was to pump water from the tin mines of Cornwall to prevent them from flooding.

Newcomen's engine used the power of atmospheric pressure, rather than steam pressure,

to do its work. At the top of the engine was a rocking beam, connected at one end by way of metal rods, to a pump deep in the mine. The other end of the beam was linked to a piston inside a steam cylinder. When the piston rose, steam from a boiler entered the cylinder beneath it. Water was then sprayed into the cylinder to condense the steam. The condensed steam took up far less space than the steam had done when it entered the cylinder, and this created a partial vacuum below the piston. Atmospheric pressure forced down the piston and the beam rocked, pulling up on the pump rods and lifting water from the mine.

The atmospheric engine was an almost immediate success, and within a few years it was in use at mines throughout Europe. One of its main advantages, apart from the fact that there was no other machine that could do the same job so well, was that it was relatively simple to build. Its major disadvantage was that it required a vast amount of coal to keep it running.

Watt's first experience of steam-engines came in 1763, when he was asked by Glasgow University to repair their working model of a Newcomen engine.

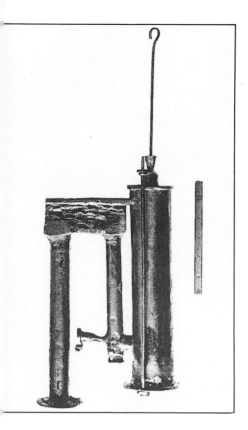

This is the original model Watt made of his separate-condenser engine. It is rather crudely built, but it worked well enough to convince Watt that his ideas were correct.

The model Newcomen engine at Glasgow University would only work for a few strokes before stopping. Also, just like the full-sized engines, it burned a lot of coal. While he was repairing the model, Watt realized why it needed so much fuel. The spray of water which condensed the steam also cooled down the cylinder, so that on the next stroke of the piston much of the steam was used in re-heating the cylinder.

Watt grappled with the problem of how to keep the cylinder at a high temperature while still using cold water to condense the steam. He must have thought about it constantly until the solution came to him in a flash of inspiration: the steam could be condensed in a separate chamber connected to the engine's cylinder. Steam would flow into the chamber until it had all condensed and the engine could continue working without the cylinder cooling down and having to be re-heated during each stroke.

In order to test his idea, Watt quickly built a model of his separate-condenser engine. It was a crude machine, made out of tin, but it was good enough to show him he was right. During the next few years, Watt worked to improve his new engine. He suffered setbacks and disappointments and might have abandoned the task had it not been for the support of Dr John Roebuck.

Roebuck had, in 1760, set up the first ironworks in Scotland. He had an interest in chemistry and through this had got to know Watt's friend Joseph Black. Thinking that a meeting might benefit both Watt and Roebuck, Black introduced the two men. As a result, in 1769 Roebuck agreed to buy a two-thirds share in Watt's steam-engine improvements and to pay for them to be patented. When he entered into his partnership with Roebuck, Watt had never built a full-sized steam-engine, nor seen a real Newcomen engine at work.

Newcomen's atmospheric engine

Thomas Newcomen was born in Dartmouth, Devon, in 1663. He became an ironmonger and blacksmith and, as part of his business, visited the local tin mines to sell tools. On these visits, he learned of the problem of pumping water from the mines to prevent them flooding.

In some mines, pumping was carried out using a steam pump, invented by a man called Thomas Savery. However, Savery's pump used two boilers mounted side-by-side and it was very dangerous. Although the steam pump was abandoned, Savery's patent protected the rights for the use of power 'produced by fire for all types of machine'. To get around this difficulty, Newcomen joined forces with Savery in 1705 and built the first real steam-engine seven years later. Newcomen's atmospheric engine – so-called because the piston was forced upward by steam pressure but lowered by atmospheric pressure – was a great success, both in Britain and abroad. Despite this, Newcomen earned very little money from his engines because of difficulties in enforcing his patent.

3 Watt's First Engines

In order to learn more about real steam-engines and their workings, in 1769 Watt helped to build a Newcomen engine at Roebuck's Carron Iron Works. He then set about building new engines to his own design. In doing so he came up against two frustrating problems. The first was that the engine parts produced by the metalworkers of the time were not accurate enough for his needs. The second was that the workmen whose task it was to assemble the engines were rather set in their ways; they were used to working on Newcomen engines and were unwilling to accept new ideas. Watt's solution to both these problems was to employ men of his own choosing – including scientific instrument-makers – to manufacture parts to the required accuracy. However, although their work was an improvement, it was still not quite good enough.

A scene inside an iron foundry. Molten iron is being run off from the furnace and cast into solid pieces.

This page from Watt's journal describes the building of his first engine at Kinneil House, Roebuck's home, in 1770.

When Watt began building his first new engine at Roebuck's house outside Edinburgh, he encountered a number of problems. These were mainly caused by the fact that his design was ahead of its time in terms of the technology which was needed to build it.

The major difficulty was in designing a seal around the piston to prevent steam from escaping. Newcomen had used a leather flap or a compressed ring of fibre as a seal, and had injected a small amount of water into the cylinder above the piston to keep it steam-tight. Watt realized that allowing the top of the piston to cool down wasted heat. So he decided to close the top of the cylinder and use the pressure of steam from the boiler, rather than atmospheric pressure, to force the piston down. This meant that a water seal could not be used.

Progress on finding a better seal came slowly. Watt experimented with various types of packing and oils to keep the small gap around the piston steam-tight. These were an improvement but the seal was still not as good as Watt required.

In 1767 Watt began working as a civil engineer. His job was to survey the routes for proposed new canals.

There were other reasons why the new engine took a long time to build. Watt was still spending some time in his instrument-making business, and Roebuck was involved in a number of schemes that distracted his attention – and his money – away from Watt's engine. It seems that Roebuck was having financial problems and was running short of money.

Since 1767, Watt had been working as a civil engineer, mainly surveying routes for proposed new canals. Manufacturing and trade were growing rapidly at the time, and it was far cheaper to transport goods by water than by horse-drawn vehicles on the roads.

In 1768 Watt travelled to London to ask the approval of Parliament for a new canal route he had surveyed, linking the Forth and Clyde rivers. The route was rejected, much to Watt's disgust. In a letter home he wrote about the House of Commons: 'I never saw so many wrong-headed people on all sides gathered together . . . I believe the Deevil has possession of them.'

The following year Watt visited London again, this time to take out a patent for his separate-condenser steam-engine. He returned to Scotland via Birmingham, a city that had become famous for the manufacture of metal goods. While he was there he met Matthew Boulton, one of the leading figures of the Industrial Revolution. Their meeting was to have an enormous effect on Watt's future.

Regent Street in London, in the eighteenth century. In 1768 Watt travelled to London in connection with his surveying work for new canals. In those days, before railways, he would have made the journey by coach.

Boulton's father was a manufacturer of ornamental metal goods. In 1764 Boulton had decided
to expand the business and had built a splendid
new 'manufactory' at Soho, about two miles from
the centre of Birmingham. It was one of the most
modern factories in Europe, employing 600
skilled craftsmen from a variety of trades.

At that time, Birmingham was in the process of
becoming a major centre of the Industrial
Revolution. In part, this was because, unlike
London, the city had no trade guilds of the kind
that had made it almost impossible for Watt to find
work some years earlier. It was also a place where
religious dissenters could set up in business
without interference. Many were manufacturers
and business people, and they were attracted by
the freedom which Birmingham offered them. As
a result, the city flourished and its population
doubled between 1770 and 1800. Craftsmen and
small workshops turned out a vast range of
products, many of which were of high quality.

*The Soho manufactory built
by Matthew Boulton in
1864. In its day it was one of
the most modern factories in
the world.*

At his Soho manufactory, Boulton was committed to making products of good quality and design at the lowest possible price. Like Watt, Boulton also had an enquiring and inventive mind. The two men quickly became friends. In terms of business, each saw what the other had to offer. Watt realized that the Soho workers could provide the skill and craftsmanship he needed to produce his new steam-engines, while Boulton – a talented businessman – appreciated the fact that industry badly needed machines like Watt's engine to supply them with power.

The obvious course was for Watt and Boulton to become partners, but Watt was still tied by his agreement with Roebuck. When he returned to Scotland, Watt urged Roebuck to bring Boulton into their partnership. Negotiations began but Roebuck was only prepared to offer Boulton a licence to make steam-engines for three English counties. Boulton rejected the offer; his plans covered much more than just three counties. In 1769 he wrote to Watt: 'I was excited by two motives to offer you my assistance which were love of you and love of a money-getting ingenious project . . . to settle a Manufactory near to my own . . . from which Manufactory We would serve the World with Engines of all sizes.'

A view of Birmingham in about 1800. The city was one of the most important centres of the Industrial Revolution, with factories turning out a vast range of products. As Birmingham's industry grew, more and more people moved there to find work; between 1770 and 1800 the population of the city doubled.

Matthew Boulton

Matthew Boulton was born in Birmingham in 1728. His father was a manufacturer of ornamental metal goods, and Matthew joined the family business. In 1762 he built a large new factory on some open land at Soho, outside Birmingham, and employed 600 craftsmen from a variety of trades to produce a huge range of goods. He was determined to make only products of high quality, and thanks to his innovation of employing many different types of craftsmen, he was able to keep production costs down.

He is probably best known for his partnership with James Watt, which began in 1774. By 1800, Boulton and Watt had built about 500 engines. Boulton played a vital role in the partnership, gaining orders for engines, finding uses to which they could be put, and encouraging Watt to develop engines for these new purposes. He was also a good engineer. He devised a way of using steam power in the minting of coins, and a Boulton machine was in use at the Royal Mint until 1882.

Boulton was an intelligent and popular man. He was one of the founders of Birmingham's Lunar Society and was a Fellow of the Royal Society. He died at Soho in 1809.

There was little that could be done while Watt's partnership with Roebuck was still in force, and so Watt returned to civil engineering. He worked on canals – sometimes supervising their construction as well as doing the surveys – and he also made improvements to the surveying instruments he used and invented a telescopic rangefinder.

Meanwhile, Roebuck's financial difficulties were growing. He had become involved in a number of costly schemes, and the failure of some of them led to him going bankrupt in 1773. Boulton bought the major interest in the steam-engine patent, and Watt dismantled his experimental engine and had it shipped to Birmingham.

For a time Watt continued his surveying work. While he was surveying part of Scotland's Great Glen, he received news that his wife was very ill. He hurried home to find that she had died while giving birth to their second child. He became very unhappy. To his friends he complained bitterly about Scotland, its weather, his work and how little he was paid for it. When he had finished the jobs he had been hired to do, Watt decided to leave the 'cursed country' of Scotland. In 1774 he headed for Birmingham.

A view of a canal in the mid-eighteenth century, showing the locks which were used to level out the slopes. Part of Watt's job as a surveyor was to plan the routes for new canals and decide where locks should be placed.

When Watt arrived in Birmingham, Boulton lent him his former home to live in, and encouraged him to restart work on improving the steam-engine. Since Watt's earlier attempts at making steam-tight seals for the piston, a new development had taken place which was to be of enormous benefit. It was not in the field of engine-building, but in the manufacture of cannons.

In France in 1773, an enquiry had been set up to find out why cannons were blowing up in the faces of French gunners. This was happening so frequently that the soldiers were more afraid of their own cannons than those of their enemies. A French army officer visited England to find out about ways of making safer cannons, and among the people he met were John and William Wilkinson, who had an iron foundry near Coalbrookdale, Shropshire.

Coalbrookdale, Shropshire, in the eighteenth century. During the Industrial Revolution, this town on the River Severn became an important centre for ironworking and other industries.

Eighteenth-century cannons. Thanks to an innovation by John Wilkinson, who had an iron foundry at Coalbrookdale, cannons could be made with an accurate cylindrical bore. Wilkinson's technique was then applied to the manufacture of cylinders for Watt's steam-engines.

John Wilkinson decided to try and solve the problem, and a year later he developed a completely new method of boring cannons. He cast the gun as a single, solid piece and then laid it horizontally in a supporting frame. A cutting tool was then attached to a Watt steam-engine and, as the engine turned, the cutting tool was moved forward slowly. A guide bar ensured that the cutting tool did not move off-centre during the boring and this meant that the barrel was almost perfectly cylindrical. By 1775 Wilkinson had made a machine that could bore engine cylinders. This invention meant that Watt's problem of keeping his cylinders steam-tight was solved. At last he was able to use an accurate cylinder.

A copper mine at Camborne, Cornwall. A great deal of Boulton and Watt's early business came from mines like this, which needed steam-engines to pump water from below ground to prevent them from flooding.

Boulton now persuaded him to build two full-sized engines, one for use at John Wilkinson's ironworks and the other at a coal-mine near Dudley in the West Midlands. Despite a few early problems, the engines soon proved their worth. A Watt engine was able to do as much work as a larger Newcomen engine, and it used only one-third as much coal. Within three years of Watt's arrival in Birmingham, several of his engines were at work in parts of Britain as far apart as Scotland and Cornwall.

It was in Cornwall that some of the best opportunities for Boulton and Watt's business were to be found. Many of the tin and copper mines were at risk from flooding, and the coal to power the Newcomen pumping engines had to be brought into the county at great expense.

The partners received many enquiries from mine-owners who were eager to cut the cost of pumping their mines, and it was not long before Watt travelled to Cornwall to supervise the building of his first engine there. The local mine engineers were suspicious of him at first. They had a great deal of experience of Newcomen engines and believed they knew all there was to know about pumping. However, Watt's engines soon won them over.

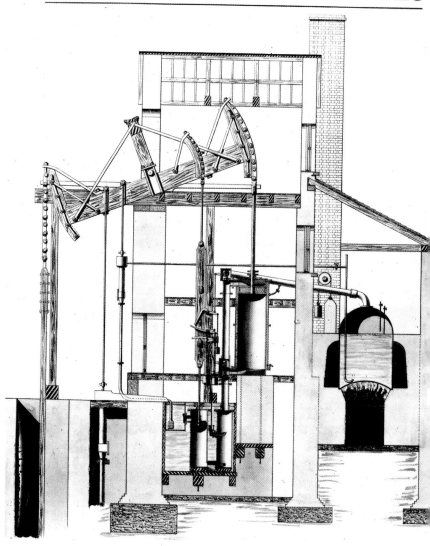

JAMES WATT 1788
SINGLE ENGINE FOR DRAINING MINES

A mine-pumping engine built by Watt in 1788. At first, many mine engineers were suspicious of Watt's engines; they were used to working with the Newcomen type and believed they knew all there was to know about steam-engines. However, Watt's engines were more powerful and much more economical to run, and the engineers soon began to use them.

Inside a mine in the eighteenth century.

Despite the fact that the business was highly profitable, Watt became deeply worried about money. Boulton had recently borrowed sums of money by offering engine royalty payments as security for a loan. This made Watt very anxious; he convinced himself that the business would go bankrupt and he would be ruined. Even though Watt wrote his partner many letters concerning his fears, Boulton seems to have been very patient and understanding.

The royalties which troubled Watt so much were, in fact, the only way in which the business was paid. When an engine was ordered by a mine-owner, Boulton and Watt supplied the technical drawings and the skill and knowledge required. The mine-owner bought the parts direct from foundries such as Wilkinson's and employed local men to build the machine. Only a few small parts which needed to be made very accurately were produced at Soho. The payment to Boulton and Watt was calculated on the savings that the mine-owner would gain by using a Watt engine instead of a Newcomen one.

In Cornwall, the comparisons between the different engines were not always straightforward, as Watt engines were often used to pump water from deeper mines than could be pumped with Newcomen engines. In these cases, Watt worked out how much a Newcomen engine would cost to run if it were possible to build one large enough to do the work. The mine-owners mistrusted Watt's complicated calculations; one even threatened to appeal to Parliament but the threat came to nothing. Watt did little to hide his contempt for such men, hinting that they were little better than thieves who were trying to pick his pocket.

While Watt was overseeing the construction of his engines, Boulton was busy too. He saw how rapidly industry was growing and he knew that he and Watt could supply the ingredient to help it grow even faster – power.

The house at Harper's Hill where Watt lived after his move to Birmingham in 1774.

As the Industrial Revolution advanced, factories sprang up in which products were made by machines rather than by hand. What these factories needed was a source of power to drive their machines. Some mills and factories used horses, which walked around a circular track pushing a yoke to turn the machinery through a series of gears. Others drew their power from river water. Water-wheels were used to change the flowing movement of the river into rotary (turning) motion for the machines.

During the early years of the Industrial Revolution, factory machines were often powered by water-wheels that were turned by the flow of water in fast-moving rivers.

However, there was a limit to the amount of power that horses could supply, and sites that were suitable for water-wheels were becoming harder to find. What is more, many manufacturers wanted to build their factories in areas that were close to the raw materials and labour they needed, and such sites were not necessarily close to usable rivers. Clearly, steam-engines would enable the manufacturers to build factories away from rivers, and Boulton was aware of this. As he said: 'I sell here Sir what all the world desires – POWER.'

Watt's engines were designed to provide 'up-and-down' (reciprocating) motion which was necessary for pumping mines but of little use for driving factory machines. Boulton wrote, urging him to think about adapting the design to produce 'round-and-round' (rotary) motion. He added: 'There is no other Cornwall to be found.'

Where there was no river suitable for driving a water-wheel, factories frequently used horses for power. As the horses moved around in a circle, they turned the central column. This rotary motion was then transferred to the factory machines through a series of gear wheels.

Right *The Boulton and Watts Soho works, Birmingham, in the nineteenth century.*

Below *One of Watt's first rotary engines. The up-and-down motion of the beam was converted into round-and-round motion by the 'sun-and-planet' gear attached to the centre of the large flywheel.*

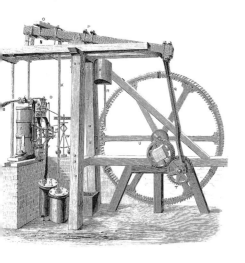

On his return to Soho, Watt began work on an engine for use in mills and factories. His first design was similar to his pumping engines. Instead of the pump at one end of the beam, however, he connected a flywheel and a shaft. They were joined to the beam by a connecting rod and a crank. The main drawback was that the crank had already been patented by a rival steam engine builder and, although the patent would probably not have been upheld if challenged in court, Watt decided to find another solution. He devised what is called an epicyclic, or 'sun-and-planet', gear. It was more complex than a crank but it worked very well, and Watt continued to use it even after the patent for the crank had run out.

At around the same time Watt also introduced another modification to his engine. He made the working cylinder 'double-acting', which means that steam was allowed into the cylinder alternately above and below the piston and condensation took place on both the up-stroke and the down-stroke of the piston. This change almost doubled the amount of power supplied by the engine.

The double-acting engine

In 1781, Watt made an important breakthrough in the design of his steam-engine. Until that time, the engine had provided power only on the down stroke; as the piston was forced down in the cylinder, it pulled down one end of the beam and raised the other end. In the double-acting engine, however, steam was allowed into the cylinder and condensed first on one side of the piston and then on the other. This produced twice as many power strokes and so almost doubled the amount of power available from an engine.

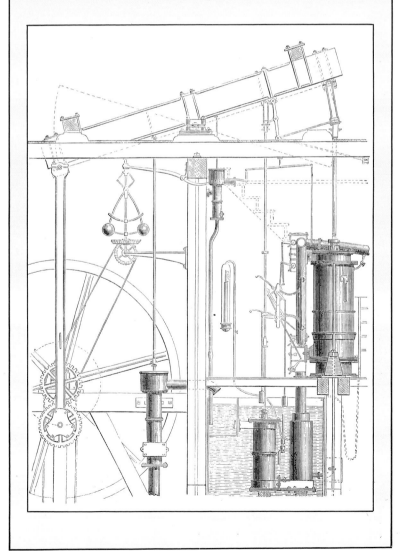

The double-acting cylinder forced other changes to be made. In earlier engines, the piston had been connected to the beam by a chain. Now Watt had to design a linkage that would both push and pull, and would move up and down vertically inside the cylinder's steam-tight seal. He came up with what he called 'parallel motion' linkage, in which the piston rod was kept upright by means of a series of joints arranged in a geometrical pattern. No doubt his instrument-making experience helped him to calculate the precise arrangements of the joints. Watt himself was pleased with the design, saying that he was '. . . more proud of the parallel motion than of any other mechanical invention I ever made.'

Watt's new engine was a huge success. One of the first to be built was installed at the Albion Mill near London's Blackfriars Bridge. It drew admiring visitors from far and wide. However, it also attracted the hatred of rival mill-owners, who suggested that the Albion Mill was trying to set up a monopoly and force up the price of flour. In fact, thanks to Watt's engine, the mill was able to cut the cost of grinding corn by more than 30 per cent.

With the introduction of the steam-engine to factory and mill work, Boulton and Watt had to devise a new method of calculating how much they charged for their engines. What was needed was a unit of measurement to define the rate at which an engine could work. Watt thought about the way horses were used to provide power in some mills, and calculated that one horse could raise 33,000 pounds (15,000 kg) by 1 foot (0.305 m) in 1 minute. This became the standard measurement of 1 'horsepower'. The partners were then able to say how much work their engines could do in terms of horsepower. They charged their new customers a royalty of £5 per horsepower (£6 in London).

Watt invented a 'governor' to control the speed of his steam-engines. As the central spindle turns faster, the balls swing outwards, pulling down the collar (E) which closed a damper (T), reducing the power.

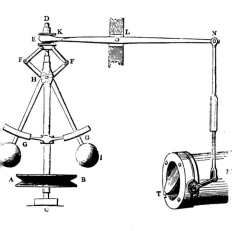

The Albion Mill near Blackfriar's Bridge, London. It was here that one of Watt's first double-acting engines was installed.

Although the idea of comparing the power of machines and horses was not new, Watt was the first person to arrive at a figure that could be used in almost any situation. He was also an innovator in other ways. In a sense, he was forced to find new ways of doing things because he refused to trust other people's ability and insisted on doing a lot of work himself. He designed most of the parts supplied by the Soho factory – a huge task in itself because almost every engine was different and was specifically tailored to the customer's needs. To help him make the calculations involved in the design, Watt used a slide rule; he seems to have been the first engineer to do so. Until the invention of the electronic calculator, the slide rule was an important tool for engineers.

The house at Heathfield, near Birmingham, where Watt spent much of his later life.

Watt was not the only engine builder of his time, but he was without doubt the most innovative. Because of this, his designs were often copied by unscrupulous rivals, and his patents were frequently challenged in court.

The patents taken out by the partners described their engines in very broad terms, and this made it difficult for other builders to construct any improved type of steam-engine without breaking the law (governing patents). To add to this, although Boulton and Watt could not hope to supply all the engines that people wanted, they refused to grant licences to other manufacturers to build Watt engines. Some 'pirate' builders did so anyway, and whenever the partners discovered this they demanded royalties from the mine- or mill-owner and attempted to stop the builder by taking legal action against him. Other owners avoided potential trouble by buying outdated Newcomen engines, even though they cost much more to run.

Many of those who challenged the patents were from Cornwall and, after 1790, a large part of Watt's time was spent in defending his patents. Eventually the partners were successful, and in 1799 their patents were upheld, not least because they brought together a large number of respected scientists to testify for them. Even though the patents had only a year to run, the decision was worth a large amount of money in royalties because many owners had been withholding payment until the legal argument was settled.

Watt's major interest was his work in engine building and other engineering work, and he had little time for pastimes such as music and painting. His favourite form of relaxation was conversation with people who shared his interests. He was fortunate that in Birmingham there was a group of such people, called the Lunar Society. At their meetings the 'lunatics', as they sometimes called themselves, discussed the latest scientific and industrial developments. Boulton was one of the

James Watt and some of his fellow members of the Lunar Society. This group included a number of the leading names in eighteenth-century science and industry.

The eminent scientist Joseph Priestley. He moved to Birmingham in 1781 and soon became a member of the Lunar Society.

most important members of the Society; others included Josiah Wedgwood, the famous pottery manufacturer, and Erasmus Darwin, the grandfather of the naturalist Charles Darwin, author of *The Origin of the Species*.

Joseph Priestley, England's leading chemist, had been a member since 1781. His views were very liberal for the time – he supported the French Revolution and the Americans' struggle for independence, and was also a minister of the non-conformist Unitarian Church. In 1791 riots broke out in support of 'Church and King', and mobs destroyed dissenters' meeting places and burned down Priestley's house. Many of the Lunar Society members shared Priestley's views and feared that their houses would be next. The rioting continued for three days, during which loyal employees guarded the Soho factory with muskets. Priestley left, first for London, and then emigrated to America, and the Lunar Society gradually declined.

During the 'Church and King' riots in Birmingham in 1791, Joseph Priestley's house was attacked by an angry mob. Priestley was a target for the rioters because he was a leading religious dissenter and supported the French Revolution.

Watt and other members of the Lunar Society became interested in the possible medical benefits of several newly-discovered gases. This cartoon shows the effects of one such gas – nitrous oxide, or 'laughing gas' – on the audience at a scientific lecture.

Through the 'lunatics', Watt became interested in the use of certain newly-discovered gases in medicine. He designed a machine to manufacture the gases and this was built at the Soho Works. Watt had a personal interest in finding out if inhaling gases such as oxygen, carbon monoxide or carbon dioxide could cure certain illnesses. His son by his second marriage, Gregory, suffered from the lung disease tuberculosis, from which he eventually died. Unfortunately, the gases proved to be of no use for curing disease, although one, nitrous oxide (or 'laughing gas'), was later used as an anaesthetic.

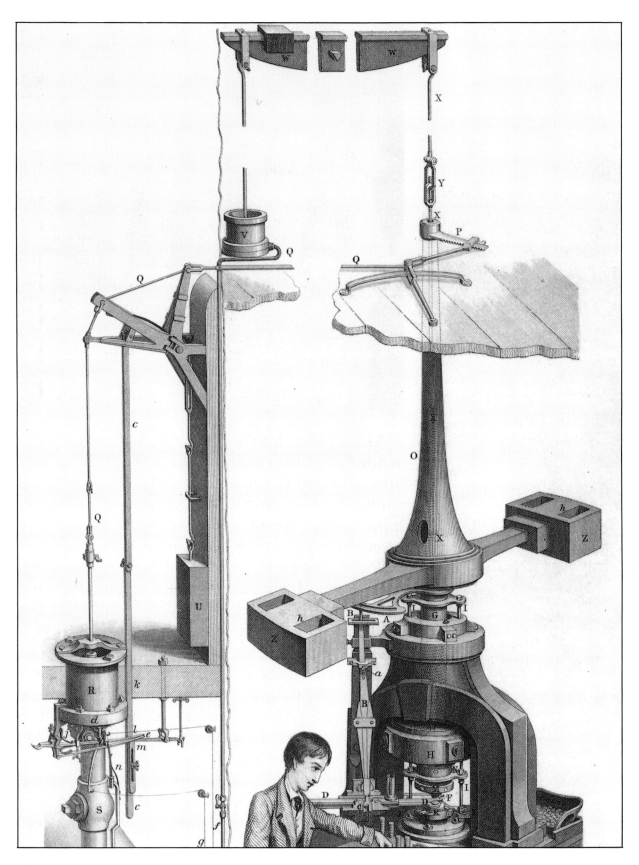

A portrait of James Watt in later life.

Opposite *The machine invented by Matthew Boulton for making coins at the Royal Mint. The invention was a great success and brought Boulton further fame.*

As they grew older, Boulton and Watt gradually handed over the running of their business to their sons. Boulton never really retired, but turned his mind to other schemes including the minting of coins using steam power. This venture was successful and brought him further fame.

Watt, however, decided to enjoy his retirement. He travelled with his second wife, and was treated as a celebrity wherever he went. His work had already been recognized by his fellow scientists in 1785, when he was made a Fellow of the Royal Society, England's most important scientific institution. To keep his mind active he experimented with a machine he had invented to copy sculptures. He also re-learnt German, which he had first learnt years earlier.

He remained alert and active and outlived most of his old friends, including Boulton, Black and Robison. In 1819, at the age of 83, Watt died following a short illness.

Throughout his life Watt was, by nature, a cautious man. He worried frequently about his health and about money, and was prone to bouts of depression. Yet, despite these factors which could have held him back, he had a highly enquiring mind and was very knowledgeable about subjects in many fields – especially science. Above all he was extraordinarily inventive.

There is little doubt that from 1774, when Watt moved to Birmingham, Matthew Boulton played an important part in his engineering achievements. As a devoted friend, Boulton was endlessly understanding and considerate; as a businessman (or, as we might call him today, an entrepreneur) he encouraged Watt's efforts and directed him towards new and profitable ventures.

Watt's workshop at his house in Heathfield. It was here that he experimented with his sculpture-copying machine.

The Cornish engineer Richard Trevithick. Although many other engine builders were challenged in the law courts by Boulton and Watt, Trevithick was largely ignored. He concentrated on using steam at a higher pressure than in Watt's designs, which made it possible to build smaller, cheaper and more powerful engines.

We shall never know how much Watt would have achieved without Boulton's help; with it, he became the best engineer of his time.

He has sometimes been accused of holding up technological progress by means of the broad nature of his patents. There may be some truth in this, although the evidence is far from clear-cut. While the partners were fighting many other engine builders in court, the Cornish engineer Richard Trevithick remained largely unchallenged. His idea was to use steam at a higher pressure than in Watt's engines, and he showed that this made it possible to build engines that were smaller and cheaper to run. Trevithick

Watt's document-copying press. The press used a special ink. A document written in this ink could be copied by pressing it on to thin absorbent paper. This made a mirror image which could be read from the reverse side.

went on to build steam locomotives, which would have been impossible with the huge beams and heavy ironwork of Watt's engines. It seems likely that if Boulton and Watt had challenged Trevithick this important development would have been delayed.

In 1809 Trevithick built a small circular railway at Euston Square, London, to demonstrate the power of his steam locomotive.

Richard Trevithick and the steam locomotive

Born near Redruth, Cornwall, in 1771, Trevithick became a mining engineer. He invented a pumping engine that was powered by water pressure, but is better remembered for the high-pressure steam-engine he built at Coalbrookdale in 1802. Steam was heated to a higher temperature than in Watt's engine, and the steam pressure was considerably higher.

Other inventors had been trying to build steam-powered road carriages, but Trevithick realized that his engine would be more useful as a means of powering a locomotive. In order to win a bet, Trevithick built a locomotive at the Pen-y-Darren ironworks in Wales which successfully pulled a train weighing 15 tonnes. When fully loaded, it moved at 8 kilometres per hour. His engine was also used as a dredging machine when he worked on the construction of a tunnel under the River Thames in 1806.

In 1816 Trevithick travelled to Peru, where his engine was introduced in the country's silver mines. When he returned to Britain after 11 years away, he had been practically forgotten, and he died almost penniless in 1833. However, his engine was a vital step in the development of steam railways.

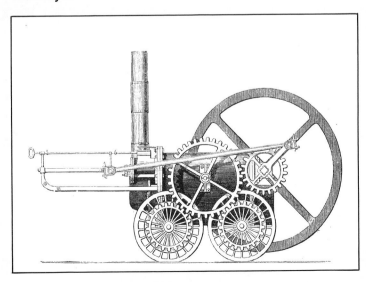

The steam locomotive built by Trevithick at Coalbrookdale in 1802. Notice that the ironwork is much lighter than that used in Watt's engines and there is no large wooden beam.

The opening of the Canterbury and Whitstable Railway in 1830. If Trevithick had been challenged in court over the steam-engine patents held by Boulton and Watt, the development of railways in Britain might have been delayed.

On the other hand, all of the 'pirates' who did infringe the partners' patents had gained their knowledge of steam power by building and maintaining Watt engines. In this way Watt could be said to have taught the engineers of his day.

Watt was an innovator in fields other than steam power. His sculpture-copying machine was one example. Another was the press he invented for copying documents. He devised it as a means of keeping track of the vast amount of paperwork that the business created – not least in the form of countless letters between the partners, who were often working away from Soho. The press used a special ink invented by Watt. When a letter was written using the ink, a copy could be made by pressing a sheet of damp, absorbent paper on to the letter. This made a mirror image of the original which could be read from the reverse side if the copy paper were thin enough. The partners began selling the press and the ink to other people and it became the standard method of copying letters until the invention of the typewriter and carbon paper.

All in all, it is probably true to say that Watt was an excellent solver of problems rather than an out-and-out genius. His success came from his ability to combine the skills of an instrument-maker with those of an engine builder, and in doing so he became the first true mechanical engineer. Genius or not, his achievements were remarkable, and they paved the way for Britain to become the world's first industrial nation.

Steam still has a part to play in generating power. In a nuclear power station, like this one in France, heat from the reactor is used to turn water into steam. The steam drives turbine blades, and their spinning motion is converted into electricity by a generator.

Date Chart

1736 James Watt born at Greenock, Scotland, on 19 January.

1754 Begins training as scientific instrument-maker in Glasgow.

1755 Spends year training in London under John Morgan.

1757 Opens workshop in Glasgow.

1763 Repairs and studies model Newcomen engine.

1764 Marries Margaret Miller.

1765 Devises separate-condenser steam-engine.

1767 Begins land surveying work for new canals.

1769 Enters into partnership with Dr John Roebuck to develop separate-condenser engine. Meets Matthew Boulton in Birmingham.

1773 Roebuck goes bankrupt. Watt's wife dies in childbirth.

1774 Boulton takes over Roebuck's share in engine patent. Watt moves to Birmingham.

1776 Watt's first full-sized engines built. Marries second wife, Ann McGregor.

1777 Travels to Cornwall to build mine-pumping engines.

1780 Patents letter-copying press.

1782 Patents double-acting rotative engine.

1783 Builds first rotative engine.

1785 Elected Fellow of the Royal Society.

1791 'Church and King' riots in Birmingham.

1793 Partners start legal action against patent infringers.

1797 Studies medical effects of gases.

1799 Engine patents upheld.

1804 Starts work on sculpture-copying machine.

1809 Death of Boulton.

1819 Watt dies on 25 August.

Books to Read

Age of Steam (Kingfisher Explorers, 1986)

Connections by James Burke (Macmillan, 1978)

James Watt and the Power of Steam by Andrew Nahum (Wayland, 1981)

Manufacturing Industry by Robin Kerrod (Wayland, 1991)

The Colour of Steam by Derek Huntriss (Atlantic Transport Publications, 1989)

The Power Generations by Clint Twist (Wayland, 1991)

Glossary

Apprentice Someone who works for a skilled craftsman in order to learn a trade.

Atmospheric pressure The pressure exerted at the Earth's surface by the weight of the atmosphere above it.

Bankrupt A word to describe a person or business that cannot pay all of the money owed.

Boring Making or enlarging holes.

Condense To change vapour into a liquid.

Crank A device for transferring movement, consisting of a rod or arm projecting from a shaft.

Cylinder The working cylinder of a steam engine is the chamber in which steam moves the piston.

Damper A movable metal plate to reduce draught in a furnace.

Dissenters People who disagree with something. Religious dissenters, or non-conformists, refused to follow the established religion of their country.

Entrepreneur A business-person who uses his or her initiative to make money, perhaps by spotting new areas in which products can be sold.

Flywheel A heavy rotating wheel that turns the uneven strokes of a piston engine into a smooth rotary motion.

Forge A place where metal is shaped by heating and hammering it.

Foundry A workshop where metal is shaped by casting it in a mould.

Guinea An amount of money equivalent to £1.05 in today's money.

Industrial Revolution The process by which Britain and then other countries changed during the eighteenth and nineteenth centuries from being mainly agricultural to mainly industrial nations.

Monopoly The sole right to manufacture or sell something.

Natural philosophy A subject that was very like what we now call physics.

Patent A grant or permit made by a government to an inventor, giving the inventor the sole right to make, use or sell the invention for a certain number of years.

Pirate Someone who infringes a patent.

Piston A form of plunger that moves up and down inside the cylinder of an engine and compresses the vapour in the cylinder.

Royalty Payment for the use of someone else's patent or invention.

Shaft A revolving rod that transmits motion or power.

Slide rule A calculating device.

Steam-tight A word to describe a seal or joint that will not allow steam to pass through it.

Trade guild An organization set up to protect the interests of particular groups of craftsmen, such as clockmakers or stonemasons.

Vacuum A space that contains air at very low pressure. It is impossible to create a total vacuum in which the pressure is zero.

Index

Picture acknowledgements

The author and publishers would like to thank the following for allowing their illustrations to be used in this book: Mary Evans Picture Library cover, 5, 6, 7, 11, 19, 20, 22, 23, 28, 30 (top), 33, 35, 36 (both), 43; Mansell Collection 8, 27, 41, 42; Ann Ronan Picture Library 4, 9, 10, 13, 14, 18, 21, 24, 26, 29, 30 (lower), 31, 37, 38; Science Museum/Wayland 3, 25, 39, 40; Science Photo Library 45; Wayland Picture Library 12, 15, 16, 17, 32, 34, 44 (both). The cover artwork is by Richard Hook.